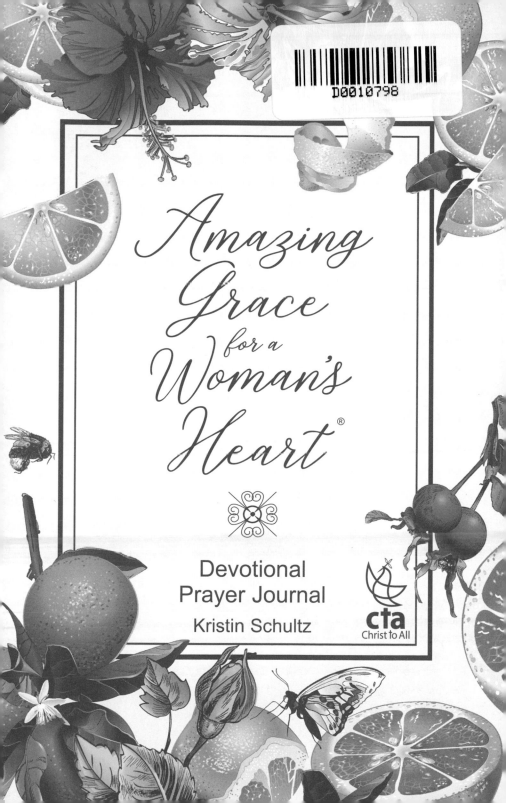

Amazing Grace for a Woman's Heart®

Devotional Prayer Journal

Kristin Schultz

cta
Christ to All

The vision of CTA is
to see Christians highly effective
in their ministry so that Christ's Kingdom
is strengthened and expanded.

Kristin Schultz

Copyright © 2022 CTA, Inc.
1653 Larkin Williams Rd.
Fenton, MO 63026
ctainc.com

Scripture quotations are from the ESV® Bible (The Holy Bible, English
Standard Version®), copyright 2001 by Crossway, a publishing ministry of
Good News Publishers. Used by permission. All rights reserved.

ISBN: 978-1-951094-10-2
PRINTED IN USA

Getting Started

We use the word *grace* a lot. We talk about God's grace. We talk about giving grace to others. We name our children and pets Grace. But have you ever stopped to meditate on grace and how God's grace to you in Jesus and his gracious gift of the Holy Spirit affect your day-to-day?

Grace can be hard to accept. Why? We want to have a hand in our salvation. We want to be able to say, "See, I'm a good person." We want to think that we can make God happy by the good things we do. We want to think God is happy with us when we treat our co-workers well or volunteer at church.

The truth is there is nothing we can do to earn God's love. No amount of good deeds will get us into heaven. Only the life, death, and resurrection of Jesus reconciles us to God, and only through Jesus can we come before God.

What a relief! Now that Jesus has done it all and no amount of Ten-Commandments-keeping will make God love us, we can share and show that grace to others, not because we have to but because we get to. Praise God for his amazing grace . . .

It is the gift of God.
Ephesians 2:8

Amazing grace! How sweet the sound
That saved a wretch like me.
I once was lost but now am found,
Was blind but now I see.

Do you remember a time when you felt God's grace was real and close? How have you experienced God's forgiveness in your life?

For all have sinned and fall short of the glory of God, and are justified by his grace as a gift, through the redemption that is in Christ Jesus.

Romans 3:23–24

Amazing Grace Every Day

Find an audio or video version of the hymn "Amazing Grace."
Listen to the entire song as a reminder that God's grace is for
you. He redeemed you through Jesus and called your
name. His grace is truly amazing.

Wretch: a despicable or contemptible person.

Think of that. Apart from Jesus, we are wretches. Sin is a stain on our life that we cannot remove. Only God's grace in Jesus removes the stain and restores our relationship with our heavenly Father. Has there been a sin in your life that you thought was too big for Jesus to forgive? How do you feel knowing that Jesus died for every sin, no matter how big or how small?

We have all become like one who is unclean, and all our righteous deeds are like a polluted garment. We all fade like a leaf, and our iniquities, like the wind, take us away.

Isaiah 64:6

Amazing Grace Every Day

Next time you are at the store or ordering online, buy an inexpensive stain remover. Put it somewhere to remind you that you are stained by your sin but that Jesus' death and resurrection has the power to wash away all your sins.

Death is not reversible. Paul writes that we are dead in our sins. Why do you think he uses death to talk about our sinful selves? Sin brings death, but Christ brings life. What do you think of when you think of being alive in Christ?

> *And you were dead in the trespasses and sins. . . . But God, being rich in mercy, because of the great love with which he loved us, even when we were dead in our trespasses, made us alive together with Christ—by grace you have been saved.*
>
> *Ephesians 2:1–5*

Amazing Grace Every Day

Paul also wrote to the church in Rome about being alive in Christ. Read what he said in Romans 6.

No one can keep God's Law perfectly. Why did God give the Israelites the Law? Can you ever win God's favor by "being good"? Write what it means to you that grace and truth came through Jesus Christ.

For from his fullness we have all received, grace upon grace. For the law was given through Moses; grace and truth came through Jesus Christ.

John 1:16–17

Amazing Grace Every Day

Write the Ten Commandments on a piece of paper. Then pray over these laws, and thank Jesus that your salvation is found in him alone as your Savior. Give praise to the Lord for his grace, truth, and acceptance of you!

Make a list of the times you can remember that you gave of yourself for someone else. As selfless as we might be, Jesus gave up everything, including his own life, in order to repair our relationship with God. How does knowing that he loves you that much make you feel?

I have been crucified with Christ. It is no longer I who live, but Christ who lives in me. And the life I now live in the flesh I live by faith in the Son of God, who loved me and gave himself for me.

Galatians 2:20

Amazing Grace Every Day

Jesus gave up himself for you. You, too, have opportunities to give of yourself for others. Think of one person you can serve today, and then do it!

The Lord has promised good to me,
His Word my hope secures;
He will my shield and portion be
As long as life endures.

What promises has God both made
and kept in your life?

And the Word became flesh and dwelt among us, and we have seen his glory, glory as of the only Son from the Father, full of grace and truth.

John 1:14

Faithful Promises Every Day

Of all the ways that God keeps his promises in our lives,
the greatest promise he kept was sending his Son,
Jesus, to be our Savior.

We put a great deal of energy into collecting and keeping temporary things—books, clothes, cars. Why do we work so hard for things that won't last? What does it mean that God's Word does not pass away? How does that affect how you live every day?

Heaven and earth will pass away, but my words will not pass away.

Matthew 24:35

Faithful Promises Every Day

As you put on your shoes today, remind yourself that those shoes—along with everything else in your closet—are temporary. Thank God for his permanent words of love for you.

Do you have a wish list on the Amazon site? Do you know someone who does? Think about that. You can save the things you want to a special place so that you don't forget what you wanted! We are told we need to have this or that or to take this vacation or that trip. How does knowing that Jesus, the Good Shepherd, provides for you change how you look at your relationship with things?

The LORD is my shepherd; I shall not want.

Psalm 23:1

Faithful Promises Every Day

Spend an hour or so clearing out some of your stuff.
Pack it up and donate it to those in need.

God not only promises to provide for what you need but also gives you good things. List three good things God has given you, and then write down why they are blessings in your life.

What father among you, if his son asks for a fish, will instead of a fish give him a serpent?

Luke 11:11

Faithful Promises Every Day

Draw a fish on a piece of paper and keep it with you
all day to remind you that God gives you everything
you need.

We know we can trust God to provide all we need, but we still tend to rely on ourselves. Has there been a time when you had no choice but to trust God's provisions? How did it feel to completely rely on God? What did you learn?

The jar of flour was not spent, neither did the jug of oil become empty, according to the word of the LORD that he spoke by Elijah.

1 Kings 17:16

Faithful Promises Every Day

Read the story of Elijah and the widow of Zarephath in 1 Kings 17:8–16. Let the story remind you that God has provided for his people for centuries, just as he provides for you today.

Through many dangers, toils, and snares
I have already come;
His grace has brought me safe thus far.
His grace will lead me home.

When has God shown you grace, mercy, and deliverance? Were you able to see it that moment, or did it take some time to recognize it?

Let us then with confidence draw near to the throne of grace, that we may receive mercy and find grace to help in time of need.

Hebrews 4:16

Strong Deliverance Every Day

Are you currently in a time of need? Keep an eye out today for ways God is working to show you mercy in this difficult time.

America is an anxious nation. We are anxious about the future, anxious about safety, anxious about our health, and anxious about our children. God tells us that we don't need to be anxious. Though there may be trouble, he is gracious to hear and deliver us. How does this promise affect how you see the world and the future?

Do not be anxious about anything, but in everything by prayer and supplication with thanksgiving let your requests be made known to God.

Philippians 4:6

Strong Deliverance Every Day

Write out your prayers today, and then speak them aloud, trusting God to hear and answer them.

Refuge: a condition of being safe or sheltered from pursuit, danger, or trouble.

If God is your refuge, how does he keep you safe and sheltered? Who or what is pursuing you and threatening danger or trouble?

_____

_____

_____

_____

_____

_____

_____

God is our refuge and strength, a very present help in trouble.

Psalm 46:1

_____

_____

_____

_____

_____

_____

Strong Deliverance Every Day

Draw your idea of a refuge or a fortress. Post it on a
bathroom mirror or put it by your bed as a reminder that
your heavenly Father shelters you from pursuit, danger,
and trouble.

What is the first thing you do when facing difficulty? Do you turn to knowledge and try to learn as much as you can about the problem so that you can fix it? Do you turn to a glass of wine "to relax"? Do you lash out in anger? God tells us to call on him, and he will be our rest. Compare and contrast times when you called on God and times when you didn't.

Call upon me in the day of trouble; I will deliver you, and you shall glorify me.

Psalm 50:15

Strong Deliverance Every Day

Just as you call on God in your day of trouble, call a friend who is hurting or struggling. Encourage her by praying with her.

There are many forces at work in our world. Jesus tells us that the thief comes to steal and destroy, but that he, Jesus, brings abundant life. How do you see people's lives stolen and destroyed by the enemy? What does an abundant life look like?

The thief comes only to steal and kill and destroy. I came that they may have life and have it abundantly. I am the good shepherd. The good shepherd lays down his life for the sheep.

John 10:10–11

Strong Deliverance Every Day

A first-century shepherd was in charge of protecting sheep and keeping them safe. Read John 10:1–18; meditate on how Jesus is our Good Shepherd.

Yes, when this flesh and heart shall fail
And mortal life shall cease,
Amazing grace shall then prevail
In heaven's joy and peace.

Life on this earth is not forever. We will
all die. What do you think of when you think
of the end of this life?

*Even though I walk
through the valley
of the shadow of
death, I will fear
no evil, for you are
with me; your rod
and your staff, they
comfort me.*

Psalm 23:4

Everlasting Assurance Every Day

Perhaps you have lost someone close to you and have felt the sting of death in your life. Read Psalm 23:4 again, and focus on the comfort God gives, even in the face of great sorrow.

Jesus' resurrection changed the world. All who trust in Jesus will have eternal life. How does believing in the resurrection change how we view death? How is our message about death different from the world's messages?

Since we believe that Jesus died and rose again, even so, through Jesus, God will bring with him those who have fallen asleep. . . . And so we will always be with the Lord. Therefore encourage one another with these words.

1 Thess. 4:14–18

Everlasting Assurance Every Day

How do you want to be remembered? What do you want people to say about you when you die? Pray for the people God has put in your life with whom you can share the Gospel.

God so loved the world. The entire world—everything and everyone in it. It's easy to love likable people. But God didn't send Jesus for the likable people. He sent Jesus for the world, his whole world. How does this affect how you see and interact with people?

For God so loved the world, that he gave his only Son, that whoever believes in him should not perish but have eternal life.

John 3:16

Everlasting Assurance Every Day

Pray for the people you know who do not know Jesus. Ask the Holy Spirit to work in their hearts so they, too, come to know God's love and assurance.

We make promises all the time. We make promises to ourselves, to our families, and sometimes even to God. We promise to work out more. We promise to take a vacation this year. We promise to be more disciplined in our devotional life. Unlike our human promises, God's promise of eternal life in Jesus is sure. He cannot go back on it, and he cannot abandon you. Describe how that makes you feel.

And this is the promise that he made to us— eternal life.

1 John 2:25

Everlasting Assurance Every Day

What do you think heaven will be like? Draw or write what you think it will be like to spend eternity with your Lord.

Salvation is a gift—not something we earn or take but something we're given. What is the best gift you've been given? What is the best gift you have given someone? What makes a gift special? What makes the gift of salvation special?

Since you have given him authority over all flesh, to give eternal life to all whom you have given him.

John 17:2

Everlasting Assurance Every Day

Meditate on the gift of eternal life you have been given. Praise God for his authority in your life and his rule over your heart.

When we've been there ten thousand years,
Bright shining as the sun,
We've no less days to sing God's praise
Than when we first begun.

Eternity is hard to wrap our heads around. For example, ten thousand days is about twenty-seven years. Now imagine ten thousand years! What do you think eternity with Jesus will be like?

He will wipe away every tear from their eyes, and death shall be no more, neither shall there be mourning, nor crying, nor pain anymore, for the former things have passed away.

Revelation 21:4

Eternal Life Every Day

Put a tissue in your pocket as a reminder that God will wipe every tear from your eyes and that with him there is no death. Pray for people you know who are grieving.

Eternal life comes from Jesus. As a believer, your eternal life has already begun. How does knowing you are living an eternal life that extends beyond your earthly death affect how you view your work and relationships?

I give them eternal life, and they will never perish, and no one will snatch them out of my hand.

John 10:28

Eternal Life Every Day

A circle is eternal with no beginning and no end. Draw and doodle circles on a piece of paper as you pray, thanking God for his promise of life forever with him. No one can snatch you out of his hand.

Testimony: an account or declaration.

What is your account of your life with God? What is your account of what it means to you to live as a dearly loved child? How is Jesus life?

And this is the testimony, that God gave us eternal life, and this life is in his Son.

1 John 5:11

Eternal Life Every Day

Think of someone who has been a Christian role model for you and has shown you what it means to live with eternal life from Jesus. Thank God for that person. If possible, reach out and thank that person for being that light to you.

Sometimes people assume that as Christians we have easy lives that are free from pain or struggle. We know this is not true! King David faced all kinds of disappointment and sadness in his life. How was he still able to say, "Surely goodness and mercy shall follow me all the days of my life"?

Surely goodness and mercy shall follow me all the days of my life, and I shall dwell in the house of the LORD forever.

Psalm 23:6

Eternal Life Every Day

Take a walk on a sunny day and be mindful of your shadow. Let it remind you that God's goodness and mercy also follow you and go with you. And when this life is over, you will live in God's house forever.

There are many things in life we spend our time and energy pursuing—money, relationships, material possessions, new experiences. We know, however, that God wants us to seek him. When do you find it hardest to keep your eyes on Jesus? What distracts you from keeping your focus on God?

One thing have I asked of the LORD, that will I seek after: that I may dwell in the house of the LORD all the days of my life, to gaze upon the beauty of the LORD and to inquire in his temple.

Psalm 27:4

Eternal Life Every Day

Where do you find the beauty of the Lord? In the Old Testament, the Israelites sensed God's presence in the tabernacle and, for a while, in the temple. Look online or in magazines for places—buildings or in nature—that make you think of the glory of God.

Amazing grace! How sweet the sound
That saved a wretch like me.
I once was lost but now am found,
Was blind but now I see.

The Lord has promised good to me,
His Word my hope secures;
He will my shield and portion be
As long as life endures.

Through many dangers, toils, and snares
I have already come;
His grace has brought me safe thus far.
His grace will lead me home.

Yes, when this flesh and heart shall fail
And mortal life shall cease,
Amazing grace shall then prevail
In heaven's joy and peace.

John Newton (1725–1807)

When we've been there ten thousand years,
Bright shining as the sun,
We've no less days to sing God's praise
Than when we first begun.

Anonymous

To see all of CTA's devotion books and journals, visit us at ctainc.com. You may order online or by calling 1-800-999-1874.

If this book has made a difference in your life or if you have simply enjoyed it, we would like to hear from you. Your words will encourage us!

Email: editor@CTAinc.com; include the subject line: AGR22PJ

Write: Editorial Manager, Department AGR22PJ
CTA, Inc.
PO Box 1205
Fenton, MO 63026-1205

Comment Online: ctainc.com (search AGR22PJ)